Daniel et,
Acheté par
1995, à Vienna, Virginie, U.S.A.

MW00388162

Metamorphoses

Metamorphoses

GREEK PHOTOGRAPHS

DANIEL SCHWARTZ

With 118 photographs
Introduction by Peter Levi

THAMES AND HUDSON

To Lila
Σέ ποιόν άλλον εκτός από σένα

Opposite title page

PHOTOGRAPHY – WRITING WITH LIGHT

Self-portrait with the Parthenon, Athens, 1984

Linking texts and captions translated from the German by
Judith Black.

© 1986 Thames and Hudson Ltd, London
Photographs © 1986 Daniel Schwartz

Printed and bound in Japan by Dai Nippon

It is odd how we take photographs for granted. At first all we see is the images, the things we are being told. We reconstruct them automatically as taught, reality and emotion. In this book the first things you will notice are the sea, the sea's edges, wind-scoured, salt-scoured walls, and the bare rooms of old sailors in the Greek islands. Then you will notice that the statues and their battered fragments belong to that same world. The child playing alone in the deserted square belongs to it. The truth is that the best photographs are like poems, which Philip Larkin called constructions or devices to give permanence to an emotional concept, to arouse it in others. They do not exist in any practical sense until they are looked at. They are a record that goes deeper than a diary and is more objective. It is also more subjective, and that is why one returns to it again and again, much as one returns to a favourite writer. Those who know Greece already will get to know it here through other and better eyes.

A sketch by Edward Lear or by Cotman is like a frozen moment, but a moment of illumination. That is because of the dashing, half improvised technique of old watercolourists. But it takes several minutes to paint even a sketch, and therefore the result sees more than the eye can see in any less time. A good photograph happens in a fraction of a second, but there is something classic, something oddly permanent about it. That is because the photographer had to stalk and hunt his prey before the final gunshot, and the mysteries and traditions of art had distilled themselves in his mind and in his hand. Then the work that went on in the dark room, the slow choices of image and texture, may have been obsessive and immensely skilful. In the case of Daniel Schwartz, I think genius really is an infinite capacity for taking pains. The result is a unique combination of freshness and permanence. Every scene is momentary and strange; one immediately feels both recognition and wonder.

Recognition of Greece. The time is always now but the composition descends as much from classical Italian painting as that of Edward Lear's sketches did. It is deeply thoughtful and still. It is absolutely modern, like the Eiffel Tower on its opening day or the newest Japanese train. So is the Greece one recognizes in these images. When the photographs were exhibited in Athens, one visitor said 'Yes, but where is the exhibition?' and others paused here and there and said 'I would never have noticed that.' What people expect is what they have been conditioned to expect. A photographer is like a good journalist, who makes them see a little more, but a very good photographer is like a short story writer. The process of his art is one of shaving down, reducing to essentials, and of brilliant, particular observation. Only particular and individual observations will do. Education and tourism have settled on Greece like the potent and vague cloud that hid the love-making of Zeus. It takes an effort like that of Daniel Schwartz to see clearly what we were looking for. These are the best and most Greek photographs of Greece. They are drenched in experience of Greek life.

Another Swiss photographer, Jean Mohr, has recorded unforgettable images of the texture of Greek stones, and Eliot Porter produced marvellous photographs of temples as empty as shells; we can remember from Greek films that visually dramatic quality of life the day before yesterday, and the popular architecture which was the backdrop to that life has been lovingly recorded. Daniel Schwartz's contribution is conscious of texture and of emptiness, and extremely conscious of its own medium. Sometimes it is surrealist. It is too considered to be called realist, even where it feeds on contemporary realities. It is a series of profoundly meditated works of art. If one asks of a sailor's face, 'Is it *this* sailor or *the* sailor?' the only answer is that it is both, but mostly *this* sailor. The light in the vast sky at dawn is momentary as well as monumental. A few of the photographs are playful, but with a playfulness that has been swallowed up in art, like Mozart's jokes. The most characteristic effect of all these images is a lasting amazement. He is one of those few photographers whose work one would like to hang for ever in a familiar room.

When I was first in Greece as a student, I expected the ancient mythology and religion to come to life, but that process took many years longer. What I was then amazed to discover, and at once, was the world of George Seferis, the background to his poetry, and what came to life for me was Seferis, not Sophocles. Here I see that world of Seferis again, and as if it had never been photographed before. That empty balcony, the classic head like a ship's figurehead, each looking out to sea and a labyrinth of islands, the burnt tree and the abandoned beach. He would have liked the ancient theatre with the gigantic dead matches; he had dreams like that. Of course there are always the classical monuments, but their meaning for him, and their meaning in these pictures, is not what we were taught to call classical at school. The Acropolis is the skeleton of an idea briefly lighted as the sun goes down, all but lost in a sombre landscape of storm-clouds and pine forest. It is cold comfort compared to 'Mourning Becomes Electra', the rough sketch of a head on a decaying wall or a ruined poster, among very Greek-looking drainpipes. George Seferis would have noticed that head.

The rest of the world is swiftly catching up with the squalor of a country that was reconstructed in a hurry,

but not with its numbed, idyllic beauty, and not of course with its strange antiquities. It used to be a theory among foreigners that no nation could have such a genius as the Greeks for unexpected beauty without a psychological basis in an equal genius for the most dramatic ugliness. But those who know the country better, as Daniel Schwartz does, can see the one in the other. The strangeness of a leafless grove of traffic signs takes on in his eye the force of a revelation. I suspect him of relishing, as I do, the cement works at Eleusis. He is pleased with the oddity of an awful statue prancing on the tops of trees. One cannot answer whether this is precisely beautiful or ugly. His Greece is dreamlike, and yet very much alive. His photographs have the intensity of dreams and the different intensity of life. They dissolve and disclose their meanings in the way that a dream does. They seem to comment on one another, and yet to stand alone.

One of the acid texts of photography is its ability to refresh, to make one see as if for the first time, with a new kind of sight. Sometimes the image itself may contribute: the empty ironwork balcony by the shore, the battered car between the wooden boats, or the cave at Vari. But it is also a question of accuracy, of technical skill. The boy in the Louvre called the Diadoumenos, a boy crowning himself as a winner, is a statue I have known for thirty years, but only in this photograph does one begin to be interested in the grain of the marble, and to compare him with the wonderfully coarse-grained marble of his cousin in the Ashmolean at Oxford. The cave at Vari was my first expedition in the countryside of Attica, and on the first day I failed to find it. No photograph of it has ever been published that reveals its qualities as well as this one. The carving among the stalactites and stalagmites is the self-portrait of a sculptor who suffered magical possession by the nymphs, and built them this cave sanctuary. One can read the inscription, and distinguish every detail of his chisel-marks from the work of time, both before his day and since, on the surface of the rock.

Those who know Greece most deeply will recognize Greece most freshly in the work of Daniel Schwartz. It is like a snail-trail over the stones, the visible record of a single human being and his passage. Some smoky-looking plaster on an old church is a study of light and shade, and such a scene may never be quite the same again. Restoration, repainting, new building, almost everything threatens it. The light seems to fall almost from the east, so it is not long after sunrise. Daniel Schwartz is evidently fond of working in fresh morning light. But the old place is admirably cobwebbed with grime and shadows. It is not an architect's picture, meant to show the entire design. But it is more than a detail. One has a sense of the whole building, of how it shoulders light and shadows as if it had no other purpose, and of its endurance, and of the slowness of the sun. The exhibition on which this book was based was called 'Metamorphoses'; one of the sequences in that exhibition was entitled 'Figures against Time'. Both these titles say something important about his style. The photographs, of

which his images are only the precondition, call for as much meditation from us as has gone into them. They have a long expectancy of life.

Nothing could be less like a stray snap-shot, and yet in a way they reminded me of Robert Lowell's translation of Pasternak's *The Seasons*, in which summer in a photographer's black hood blinds us with flash-bulbs, and the thunder 'takes a hundred souvenir snap-shots':

> . . . *Something in my mind's*
> *most inaccessible corners*
> *registers the thunder's illumination,*
> *stands up, and steadily blinks.*

Peter Levi
13-19 February 1986

Unfolding like a mirror image in the centre of this book is the double triptych *Parallel lives*. The conception is governed by the principle of unity in diversity, so that every sequence – each making its own individual statement – is integrated into a totality. The material is thus drawn together by means of visual links between the photographs.

As the pages are turned, and these pictures examined, far-reaching connections suggest themselves. A relief juxtaposed with a theatrical scene, for example, may give the impression of a cinematic superimposition (pp.126-7).

Each sequence in the first half of the book can be associated with one in the second. In each case the two companion pieces have some or other motif in common, or the second continues the first in another dimension of space or time.

The diptychs 'On Nature' and 'Sailor and Gorgon' both indicate the existence of a historical figure in the

consciousness of a later generation. Hölderlin and Empedocles: a kindred affinity which became poetry. The Greek folk tale still today permits the sailor to answer the Gorgon's question about the fate of Alexander: 'He lives and rules the world' (pp.26-7 and 160-61).

Time or Man. Who is really the 'Measure of all things'? Part one of this series depicts civilization taking possession of nature; part two the dissolution of artificially contrived order by the process of eternal change symbolized by the sea (pp.29-33 and 155-9).

The metamorphoses which give this book its name are many-sided. The burnt tree brings to mind a transformation myth. Prometheus and Christ exchange roles. Light brings marble to life, but freezes water. The butterfly, itself created by a metamorphosis, becomes a symbol. The author's pictures themselves become the elements of his subject-matter.

The author's diary entries allow the reader to participate in the development of the work.

LUMINOUS LANDSCAPE (*part one*)

Coast of Prasiai, Porto Raphti, 1980

Diving in the Alpheios.
My journey began on the lower reaches of this river,
behind Olympia. I looked for the ford, pushed the reeds
aside: Chloe stood on the sandbank in the haze, holding
out her fair hair. Young dogs guarded the flock on the far
bank.

Karytaina, eyrie on the clifftop. Dead afternoon hours
before drawn blinds. Only local dignitaries and heroes
of the revolution linger in the heat. The barrels of their
guns rust at their feet.

Outside Megalopolis, near the theatre, they've built a
power station. Colossal backdrop of the modern age.
Of the ruins of ancient Megalopolis, Pausanias
remarked:
'. . . the gods are always striving to create anew while
fate is . . . constantly changing everything.'

Megalopolis, 17 July 1977

I

TIDES

I/II Santorini, 1982

II

I

SEISMOGRAM

I Volcano landscape, Kameni, Santorini, 1982
II Waves and black sand, Santorini, 1982

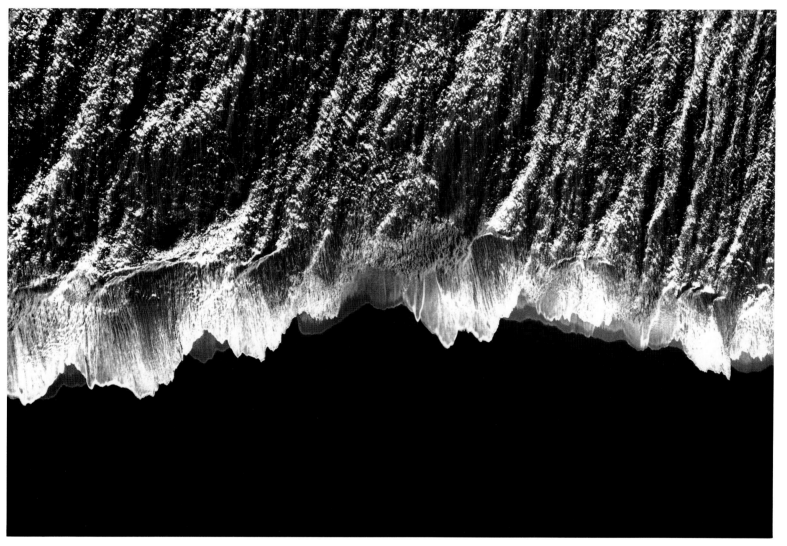

II

BIRTH OF AN ISLAND

I The Caldera, Phira, Santorini, 1982
II Interior, Phira, Santorini, 1982
III The Caldera, Phira, Santorini, 1982

I

II

III

Kythera appears.

The ship berths. Two rows of houses. A few bathers. In
sharp bends the road twists its way up to Chora. Sunday
emptiness. Soft metallic humming among the tops of the
palm trees in the square. I'm shown a place where I can
stay; the bed behind a screen.

Someone comes up the stairs. Or was it thunder that
woke me?

Viewed from the hill, the village appears in a curious
evening light. The white cuboid houses soaked in the
shining brilliance of the day. Behind the castle, lead-
coloured space. Sky and sea have vanished. The rain
begins. Dust falls with the first drops.
There's a smell of chalk and basil.

Chora, Kythera, 24 July 1977

ANDROMEDA

Kea, 1982

NIOBE

Nisyros, 1978

I

'ON NATURE' (Empedocles)

I 'Earth and Air', Fornazzo/Mt Etna, 1979
II 'Fire and Water', Mt Etna, 1979

II

THE MEASURE OF ALL THINGS *(part one)*

I The ruins of Carthaia, Kea, 1982
II The Stoa, Sanctuary of Artemis, Brauron, 1981
III The Acropolis, Athens, 1984

I

II

III

I

< FOLD OUT

ARCHITECTURAL FANTASY

I Temple of Poseidon, Sounion, 1979
II Column and chimneys, Eleusis, 1982
III Flue, mining district, Lavrion, 1978

III

II

I

LAND ART

I Domed tomb, Thorikos, 1985
II View from the Mycenaean citadel, Tiryns, 1985

II

CELESTIAL SPACE

I Leonidas monument, Thermopylae, 1981
II Tomb of Philopappos, Athens, 1984

II

I

SCENERIES

I Theatre entrance, Ancient Thera, Santorini, 1982
II The ancient theatre, Eretria, 1979

II

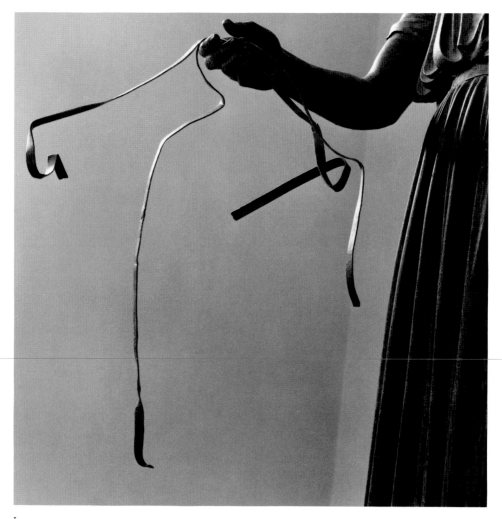

I

SIGNS OF VICTORY *(part one)*

I Arm and reins of the Charioteer, Archaeological Museum, Delphi, 1984
II The horses of Lisyppos, San Marco, Venice, 1984

II

On the headland:
Perched up in the rocky niche. Mass of stray roots.
Naked.
From the black waters far below shapes of foam escape
into nothingness.

Hollow by the village:
Someone is walking through the dry fields, treading
potsherds into the earth, swaying on crumbling stone
walls, grasping at thorns and the wind. Someone,
anyone, no longer me.

The Night Café:
Speaking – a new experience.

Chora, Kythera, 29 July 1977

IDOLS

I Burnt tree, Peloponnese, 1981
II Stage set, Epidauros, 1981

I

II

I

THE LONG WAIT OF THE CARYATIDS

I The Erechtheion, Athens, 1983
II Caryatids, Acropolis Museum, Athens, 1980

II

ARCHAIC SMILE

Aeginetan warrior, National Archaeological Museum, Athens, 1982

DIALOGUES AT THE MUSEUM

I The Argive brothers Kleobis and Biton, Archaeological Museum, Delphi, 1984
II Heads and mosaics, Archaeological Collection, Mytiline, 1983
III The Cecrops group from the west pediment of the Parthenon,
Acropolis Museum, Athens, 1983
IV Model of the Sacred District, Archaeological Museum, Eleusis, 1982

V The sculptures from the east pediment of the Parthenon, British Museum, London, 1984
VI Poseidon from Melos, National Archaeological Museum, Athens, 1983
VII Frieze panels from the Parthenon, Acropolis Museum, Athens, 1983
VIII The Charioteer, Archaeological Museum, Delphi, 1984

I

II

III

IV

V

VI

VII

VIII

He had asked a boy to buy sandals for him in the village.
His fingers struggle patiently with the hard plastic; they
scarcely respond. He doesn't want help.
The wheelchair is facing that gap in the parapet of the
terrace where a strip of the Aegean can be seen and
pennants of spray leap high into the air.
'Rhodes 1908. A life at sea. Captain for twenty-four years.'
Casually he raises his hand from the table just a little –
enough to turn the pages to Arabia, India, Hong Kong . . .
'Second World War. Italy. An explosion on board.'
In the summer he comes here, to the small neighbouring
island. The sulphur springs are supposed to bring relief.
At last the oversized bundle of washing is tied fast and
the boy, balancing the load, steers his bicycle past the
guesthouse towards the road.

Loutra, Nisyros, July 1978

A CAPTAIN'S TWILIGHT

I-VII The old spa of Mandraki, Nisyros, 1978

STABILIMENTI TERMALI DI MANDRACCHIO · NISIRO (ΕΘΕΟ)
ΦΥΣΙΚΑ ΙΑΜΑΤΙΚΑ ΛΟΥΤΡΑ ΜΑΝΔΡΑΚΙΟΥ · ΝΙΣΥΡΟΥ (ΑΙΓΑΙΟΝ)

I

II

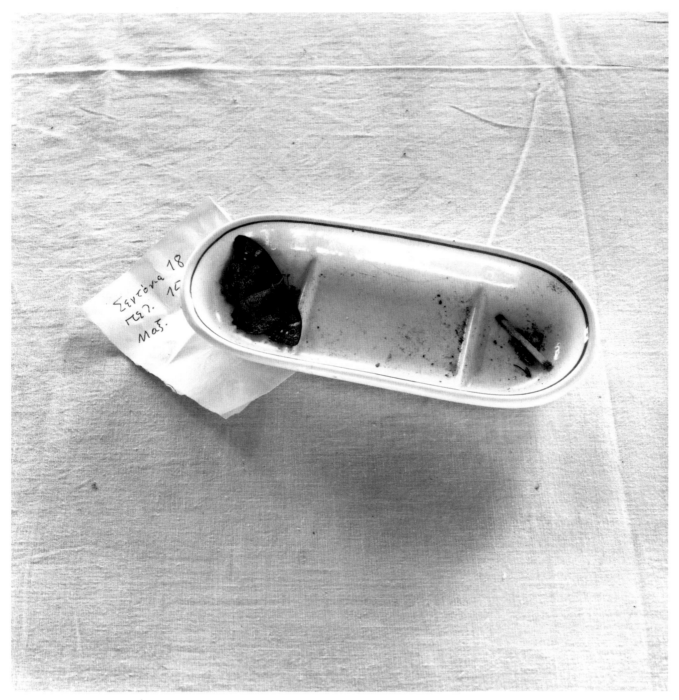

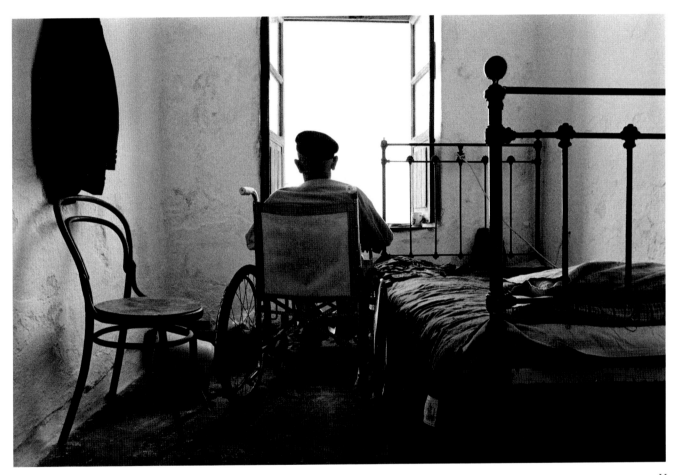

V

VI

VII

Models and mannequins abandoned. Their loneliness
etched out behind the studio equipment, the curtain, and
their little victories on the catwalk.
Back with the wounded statues which, torn from the
temples of faith, are now to justify the temples of
knowledge.
I'm struggling with the concept for my Greece
Exhibition. Few people, yet *striding* feet of marble.
Landscapes swept bare. Empty chairs. Uninhabited
buildings, wrappers of history. Intervals. Ashes in the
Archaeological Park, long after us.
Metamorphoses.

Zurich, 22/25 February 1983

SIGHTSEEING

The tomb of Agamemnon, Mycenae, 1982

I

EUROPEAN ENCOUNTER I – THE CHILDREN OF MINOS

I Hippy colony, Matala, Crete, 1975
II Festival of the Cretan community, Zurich, 1983

II

I

VARIATION ON AN HISTORICAL THEME – THE AEGEAN POMPEII

I The excavations, Akrotiri, Santorini, 1982
II Interior, Akrotiri, Santorini, 1982

I

VARIATION ON AN HISTORICAL THEME – THE GILDED AGE

I The temple of Athena Nike, Athens, 1983
II The Pnyx, Athens, 1981

I

VARIATION ON AN HISTORICAL THEME – 'OWLS' FROM EARTH

I Ancient silver mine, Lavrion, 1978
II Leadworks, Lavrion, 1980

II

III

I

II

FOLD OUT >

'PARALLEL LIVES' (Plutarch) *(part one)*

I The Athenian treasury, Delphi, 1981
II The Athenian Stoa, Delphi, 1981
III Steps of the theatre, Delphi, 1981

< FOLD OUT

'PARALLEL LIVES' (Plutarch) *(part two)*

I Unfinished hotel, Kyllene, 1981
II Concrete columns, Lamia, 1981
III Unfinished church, Macedonia, 1981

II

III

I

I

VARIATION ON AN HISTORICAL THEME – ASSIMILATION

I Corinthian Capital, Church of St John of the Column, Athens, 1984
II Classical relief, Church of St Paraskevi, Markopoulon, 1981

II

I

VARIATION ON AN HISTORICAL THEME – FOREIGN RULE

I The Golden Gate, Constantinople, 1984
II Medieval watchtower, Messogia, Attica, 1985

II

I

VARIATION ON AN HISTORICAL THEME – CLASSICAL MOTIFS

I Violin, Kythera, 1977
II Stage, 19th-century ballroom, Lavrion, 1980

II

I

EUROPEAN ENCOUNTER II – MYRON MEETS MICHELANGELO

I Piazza delle Signoria, Florence, 1977
II Illioupolis/Athens, 1984

II

CYCLADIC IDOL 'X-RAYED'

Idol from Amorgos, National Archaeological Museum, Athens, 1980

Back from Greece.

Delphi:
Strange twist of fate, that I should see my pictures
exhibited there, where years ago I was permitted my
first encounter with Hellas, first discovered an affinity.
Sensations of a journey of discovery. Pencil sketches
during pauses on the steps. On continuing the climb, a
few quick photographs – because everyone takes them.
Memories, forgotten in the archives.
By chance, the rediscovery of the old negatives. Do they
not after all reveal some artistic intent? Man's structures
and the towering limestone bow of the Phaedriades,
each complementing the other: the ideal landscape.
When I photographed the Delphic triptych much later I
didn't know that the idea had already long been formed.

Athens:
Opening day. In groups the visitors crowded from room
to room. Handshakes. Faces were looking at them: the
Aeginetan warrior, smiling; seasoned, the island
captain; unapproachably large, the transfigured Christ.
My thoughts on new pictures.
The exhibition, ever open to change.

Zurich, 16 October 1983

PICTURES AT AN EXHIBITION *(part one)*

Poster for the exhibition *Metamorphoses* (1st version), Athens, 1983

ANCIENT HERITAGE

I Fragments, Theatre of Dionysos, Athens, 1982
II Font, Cathedral of St Demetrios, Thessaloniki, 1981

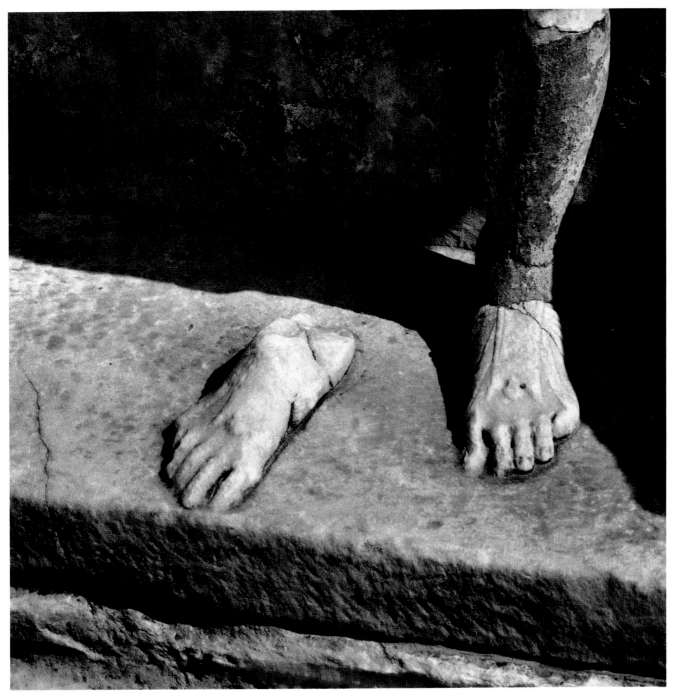

I

II

PICTURES AT AN EXHIBITION *(part two)*

Installation at the *Metamorphoses* Exhibition (1st version),
European Cultural Centre, Delphi, 1984

SEDIMENTS

I Still life with map of Greece, Zurich, 1985
II Objet trouvé, Pergamon, 1985

I

II

FIGURES AGAINST TIME

I Torso, Archaeological Museum, Pergamon, 1985
II The Diadoumenos, Louvre, Paris, 1976
III Fragment, Agora Museum, Athens, 1982
IV Relief (detail), National Archaeological Museum, Athens, 1983

V Scene from *Iphigenia in Tauris* (Euripides), Eleusis, 1981
VI The Muse, scene from *Rhesos* (Euripides?), Epidauros, 1981
VII Odysseus, scene from *Rhesos* (Euripides?), Epidauros, 1981
VIII Scene from *Epitrepontes* (Menander), Pendeli, 1982

I

II

III

IV

V

VI

VII

VIII

Still to be invented is that space between two book covers which could hold my interpretation of the 'Idea of Greece': a system to determine the order of the various sequences. What characterizes an endless chain? Each link leads on to the next and retains its own unity in spite of the encroachment. Everywhere, beginning and end.

Zurich, 3 November 1983

'MOURNING BECOMES ELECTRA' (O'Neill),

Athens, 1981

I

THE LAST PANTHEON

I Syncretic architecture, Mantineia, 1981
II Souvenirs, Nea Smyrni/Athens, 1984

THE PROMETHEAN IDEA

I Prometheus Bound, Syracuse, 1979
II The Ascension (detail), Church of St Kyriaki, Keratea, Attica, 1981

I

II

Two hours ago, still in Argolis at the orange harvest.
After the pass, sudden driving snow in the dazzling white
evening sun.
Our journey has familiar destinations – Tiryns, Mistra,
Olympia. The very last gaps in my project are to be
filled.
By the road, the church of Mantineia. Contemporary
architectural conglomeration on an historical site. The
blocks of marble, scattered across the countryside on
my first visit, now form the façade of a temple. What was
pleasing – and confusing – as a ruin now turns out to be
the foundations.
Just for once I had silently expected permanence,
constancy, but I find change. As if to spite me, the
Arcadian storm which has fascinated the eye continues
its performance. Swirling clouds are torn to pieces on
the mountainsides. Rays of light streak the evening
landscape; again and again their path sweeps the
strange monument.
I had photographed it that time on a lightless morning.
The picture's in my bag – impossible to replace. A new
wall cuts through the former line of vision. There is no
other viewpoint.

Mantineia, 11 January 1985

I

SIGNS OF VICTORY *(part two)*

I Homage to Emperor Theodosios I, relief on the base of the Obelisk, Hippodrome,
Constantinople, 1984
II The Serpent column from Delphi, Hippodrome, Constantinople, 1984

I

'THE GREAT CHURCH'

I Hagia Sophia, Constantinople, 1984
II Interior, Hagia Sophia, Constantinople, 1984

II

I

ECHOES

I Church of the Archangel, Markopoulon, 1979
II The double-headed eagle, Cathedral of St Demetrios, Mistra, 1985

I

BETWEEN HEAVEN AND EARTH

I Morning, Holy Mount Athos, 1985
II Evening, the valley of the River Pinios, seen from the Meteora monasteries, 1980

II

I

< FOLD OUT

WHITE SHADES

I Church in the Venetian fortress, Chora, Kythera, 1977
II Village and fortress, Chora, Kythera, 1977
III Agave, Chora, Kythera, 1977

III

II

THE MEASURE OF ALL THINGS *(part two)*

I Traffic signs, Hellinikon, 1984
II Mobile home, Patras, 1985
III Seaside resort, Lagonisi, 1985

I

II

III

I

'SAILOR AND GORGON' *(Greek folk tale)*

I Reflection, Vourkari, Kea, 1982
II Figurehead, Porto Raphti, 1982

II

ALIENATION – NATURE BECOMES ART

Self-portrait of the ancient sculptor Archidemos, the Nymphs' Grotto, Attica, 1984

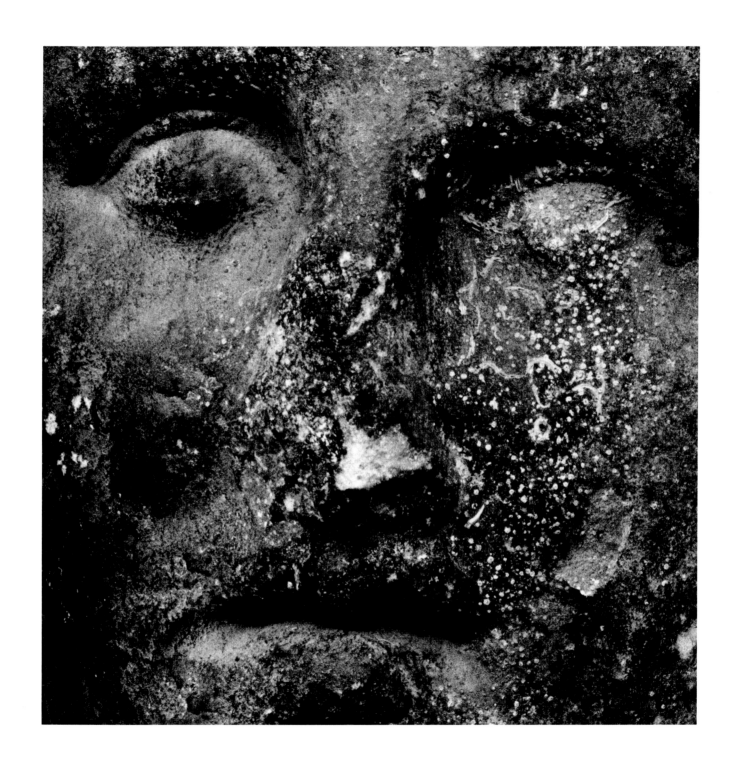

ALIENATION – ART BECOMES NATURE

Marble head from the sea at Lavrion, National Archaeological Museum, Athens, 1980

The work is completed.

One last time on the sea whose breath envelopes this, my land. Coastlines spring from the horizon, rise up into chains of hills, mountain ranges and peaks. Islands sink away, scarcely allowing one time to catch their shape, utter their names. Grey-yellow hazy pictures, ever newly-framed by the bars of the railing. In their paleness, hidden from the other passengers, my places, essence of my pictures.

They are the memories of my Greek decade.

All the photographs which could still be taken, who can count them? Yet haven't they all been thought of already?

Among the dry grass and the rubble in the mighty mussel shell of the Pergamon theatre lies a torn film – lit by the sun, developed by the rain, dried by the heat; the layers flaking, already half peeled away. Vestiges of pictures which nobody could save, which disintegrated in the element from which they came – the light.

On board, 27 July 1985

MYTHICAL GEOGRAPHY

I The 'Tailor's Island', Porto Raphti, 1979
II Mount Olympos, Farsala, 1980
III Mount Pentelikon, Merenda, Attica, 1979

I

II

III

I

PHAEACIAN VESSELS

I Boats and wrecked car, Rafina, 1984
II Nauplia, 1982

II

I

HOMAGE TO PAUSANIAS

I Varia, Lesbos, 1983
II Voula, Attica, 1983

II

LUMINOUS LANDSCAPE

Coast of Prasiai, Porto Raphti, 1983

ON PHOTOGRAPHY

Zurich, 1985

ACKNOWLEDGMENTS

The production of this book has been generously assisted by Pro Helvetia, the Swiss Council for the Arts, and the Kuratorium für Kulturförderung, Canton of Solothurn. The author wishes to thank these institutions, His Eminence The Metropolitan of Switzerland and Exarch of Europe Damaskinos, Geneva, and His Excellency The Honorary General Consul of Greece in Zurich Athanasios Ghertsos, as well as the friends who have helped in the most varied ways during the long preparation in Greece and Switzerland.

The quotation on p.7 from Robert Lowell's translation of Pasternak's *The Seasons* is reproduced from his anthology *Imitations* © Robert Lowell 1958, 1959, 1960, 1961, published in the USA by Farrar, Straus and Giroux Inc., and in the UK by Faber and Faber Ltd.

The enlargements used for reproduction are on Ilfobrom-Galerie paper.

The book accompanies an international travelling exhibition supported by Pro Helvetia, conceived and organized by Lila Zoelly-Koutalides, and mounted by the Foundation for Photography, Switzerland, at the Kunsthaus, Zurich (19 September to 30 November 1986), and in the Musée de L'Elysée/Musée pour la Photographie, Lausanne (1987), followed by a tour of the USA. The original version of this exhibition was shown in Greece in 1983-4 and at the Council of Europe, Strasbourg, in 1985.

EMBODIMENT

Hypnos, the god of sleep as night bird, Prado, Madrid; Zurich, 1985